DANGEROUS WORK!

ALLIGATOR HANDLER

THEIA LAKE

PowerKiDS press

Published in 2026 by The Rosen Publishing Group, Inc.
2544 Clinton Street, Buffalo, NY 14224

First Edition

Editor: Greg Roza
Book Design: Rachel Rising

Photo Credits: Cover, THEPALMER/iStock.com; pp. 1, 3–24 Pattern image/Shutterstock.com; p. 4 Philippe Clement/Shutterstock.com; p. 5 meunierd/Shutterstock.com; p. 7 Photomika-com/Shutterstock.com; p. 8 ADfoto/Shutterstock.com; p. 9 sylviane decleir/Shutterstock.com; p. 10 Viktor Thaut/Shutterstock.com; p. 11 Irina Montero/Shutterstock.com; p. 12 JPC-PROD/Shutterstock.com; p. 13 Design Pics/Alamy Stock Photo; p. 15 MarynaG/Shutterstock.com; p. 17 James M. Chambers/Shutterstock.com; p.18 Eric Isselee/Shutterstock.com; p. 19 Greg and Jan Ritchie/Shutterstock.com; p. 20 Robert Eastman/Shutterstock.com; p. 21 Kristina Bessolova/Shutterstock.com.

Cataloging-in-Publication Data

Names: Lake, Theia.
Title: Alligator handler / Theia Lake.
Description: Buffalo, New York : PowerKids Press, 2026. | Series: Dangerous work! | Includes glossary and index.
Identifiers: ISBN 9781499452303 (pbk.) | ISBN 9781499452310 (library bound) | ISBN 9781499452327 (ebook)
Subjects: LCSH: Alligators–Juvenile literature. | Animal handling–Juvenile literature.
Classification: LCC QL666.C925 L35 2026 | DDC 597.98'4–dc23

Manufactured in the United States of America

CPSIA Compliance Information: Batch #CSPK26. For Further Information contact Rosen Publishing at 1-800-237-9932.

CONTENTS

THRILLING WORK

Alligator handlers work with deadly animals every day. It's hard to think of a more dangerous job! Everyday activities may include feeding a lake full of hungry gators, **isolating** one for health care, and even doing daring **stunts** for crowds of people! Why would anyone even want to be an alligator handler? For the thrill!

Alligator handlers have a one-of-a-kind set of skills. They must be strong, brave, and quick thinking. They must also have a full understanding of alligators and their actions.

Could you keep your cool while surrounded by hungry alligators? If so, it might be a good job for you!

GETTING TO KNOW GATORS

There are only two species, or kinds, of alligators. Chinese alligators live near the Yangtze River in China. Mississippian or American alligators live in the southeast United States. This book will discuss the American alligator.

Alligators are large **reptiles**, and one of the world's deadliest predators. They are built for hunting! Hard scales cover their body. Their huge mouth is filled with pointed teeth! Alligators are very strong. In the wild, alligators hide and wait for animals to wander by, and quickly **ambush** them before they can react.

STAY SAFE!

Alligators are known to do a "death roll" while hunting for a meal. Once they grab on to an animal, they begin to roll in the water, ripping away part of the animal.

Alligators usually seem calm and sleepy. But they can run quicky when they want to.

ZOO WORKERS

Many alligator handlers work for zoos. The alligators and other reptiles in zoos need daily attention from specially trained workers. Alligators need to be fed twice a week. This meal often includes whole chickens!

Alligators sometimes need to be washed. Workers may use brushes to get them clean. They use hoses and brushes to clean alligator **enclosures**. Sometimes alligators need **medical** attention. Common medical needs include broken teeth and injuries from fights with other alligators.

Even smaller or younger alligators are dangerous.

ALLIGATOR FARMS

Another type of place that needs alligator handlers is reptile or alligator farms. These places can have hundreds of gators! Many also have snakes, colorful birds, turtles, and more.

Alligators aren't exactly friendly, but they can be trained. Alligator handlers at alligator farms may get hands on with their gators! They may open an alligator's mouth to show their fearsome teeth to the crowds. Some even place their hands or arms inside an alligator's mouth. Only trained handlers should try these stunts!

A large part of an alligator handler's job is to teach others about alligators.

GATOR DOCTORS

Like all animals, alligators sometimes become ill. Reptile **veterinarians** are trained to treat all kinds of reptiles, including alligators. A regular vet who treats your family pet may not have the knowledge to treat alligators.

In February 2024, workers at a zoo in Omaha, Nebraska, noticed one of their alligators, Thibodaux, was sick. A team of handlers and veterinarians carefully removed him from his enclosure and treated him. They removed 70 coins from Thibodaux's belly!

STAY SAFE!

Training to become a veterinarian is much different from the training required to be an alligator handler. Veterinarians go to college for up to 8 years. But veterinarians will need the help of handlers.

What do veterinarians do when they need to treat an alligator that's hurt—and maybe angry? They often give an alligator some medicine to make it fall asleep during treatment.

ANIMAL CONTROL AND RESCUE

Some alligator handlers work for animal control offices. They are called when an alligator shows up in someone's backyard or local pond! Sadly, officials are sometimes forced to kill dangerous alligators. Many times, alligators are placed in **nature preserves** or alligator farms.

In states where alligators are common, alligator **management** programs have teams of handlers who are called to alligator sightings. They save hurt alligators. They also teach people how to stay safe if an alligator shows up.

STAY SAFE!

Some people buy or even find baby alligators to keep as pets. Most quickly realize it's not a good choice! Often these young alligators are let go into the wild—sometimes in populated areas. This makes animal control's job even harder.

Some animal control workers keep an eye on wild alligator groups. They make sure alligator populations are healthy and not a danger to people.

TRAINING

Some people who work with alligators went to college for **zoology**. But you don't need to go to college to become an alligator hander. Reptile handling courses across the country teach people about all reptiles (alligators, crocodiles, snakes, turtles, lizards, etc.). You learn about reptile **habitats**, food, health, and much more. An adult can help you learn more about reptile handling courses near you.

However, much of the training needed to become an alligator handler comes from working with them directly.

STAY SAFE!

Jamie Bridges is the owner of the Arkansas Alligator Farm and Petting Zoo. His grandfather bought the farm in 1947. Bridges grew up on the farm, and even played with alligators when he was young. Even with his lifelong training, Bridges has been bitten by an alligator!

An alligator handler at the St. Augustine Alligator Farm Zoological Park shows a crowd of people how to control a huge alligator with no fear.

TALENTS AND SKILLS

Alligator handlers need to be brave! It takes daring to stand in the middle of a group of deadly alligators. But it takes more than that. Alligator handlers must be fit and strong. Gators can weigh up to 1,000 pounds (454 kg).

Handlers know how to read an alligator's body language. They can tell when an alligator might be hurt or upset. Alligator handlers learn how alligators act by watching and studying them.

Alligators are usually calm, but they can move fast and with little notice. Handlers must be very careful and watchful for this.

THE RIGHT JOB FOR YOU?

Becoming an alligator handler is not a common job choice. However, zoos, nature preserves, veterinarians, and animal farms all need brave, trained alligator handlers. You might even get a start as an assistant or helper at a zoo or animal farm.

Do you think you could make it as an alligator handler? Do you have bravery and strength, and do you think quick on your feet? Do you like working outside and with animals? If so, you might be a future alligator handler.

Depending on where you live, you may not have the chance to see and learn about alligators up close. Try to visit an alligator farm or zoo that allows you to learn all about these amazing reptiles.

GLOSSARY

ambush: A surprise attack.

enclosure: A living space for animals in zoos or farms.

habitat: The natural home for plants, animals, and other living things.

isolate: To put or keep something in a place that is separate from others.

management: Oversight and guidance.

medical: Having to do with treatment from a doctor.

nature preserve: An area of land where plants and animals are kept safe from damage or harm.

reptile: A cold-blooded animal with thin, dry pieces of skin called scales.

stunt: An unusual or difficult feat often performed in front of a crowd or audience.

veterinarian: An animal doctor.

zoology: The science concerned with the animal kingdom and animal life.

FOR MORE INFORMATION

BOOKS

Katz, Susan B. *Is It an Alligator or a Crocodile?* North Mankato, MN: Pebble, 2022.

Schwartz, Heather E. *Alligators: Wetland Engineers.* Minneapolis, MN: Learner Publications, 2025.

WEBSITES

National Geographic Kids: American Alligator
kids.nationalgeographic.com/animals/reptiles/facts/american-alligator
National Geographic has a lot more to say about alligators!

St. Augustine Alligator Farm Zoological Park
alligatorfarm.com
This website shows what the St. Augustine Alligator Farm has to offer visitors, including videos and informnation about alligators.

Publisher's note to educators and parents: Our editors have carefully reviewed these websites to ensure that they are suitable for students. Many websites change frequently, however, and we cannot guarantee that a site's future contents will continue to meet our high standards of quality and educational value. Be advised that students should be closely supervised whenever they access the internet.

INDEX